If You Lived at the Time of Squanto

by ANNE KAMMA
Illustrated by PAMELA JOHNSON

SCHOLASTIC INC.
New York   Toronto   London   Auckland   Sydney
Mexico City   New Delhi   Hong Kong   Buenos Aires

ISBN-13: 978-0-439-87628-5
ISBN-10: 0-439-87628-1

12 11 10 9 8 7 6 5 4 3   7 8 9 10 11/0

Printed in the U.S.A.
First printing, November 2006

For Ellen

ACKNOWLEDGMENTS

With grateful thanks to the many helpful people at the American Museum of Natural History, New York City, NY; Wayne Furman, Office of Special Collections, Research Libraries of the New York Public Library; Harry Orlyk, for the use of his extensive library on Native Americans; the staff at Bancroft Public Library, Salem, NY: Peg Culver, Julie Brown, Rebecca Brown, and Don McMorris; my editor, Eva Moore; Ellen Levine; the wonderful resources of Plimoth Plantation; Kay Crank and Margaret Waterson, Battenkill Books, Cambridge, NY; and Moondancer, for his help with *Wampanoag Cultural History: Voices from Past and Present*.

CONTENTS

Introduction 6

Who were the Wampanoag Indians? 8

What did the Wampanoag think of the Europeans? 10

Who was Squanto? 11

What was the great sickness? 12

Where did the Wampanoag live? 13

What would you wear? 16

Would you have long hair? 18

How would you take a bath? 19

Were parents strict? 20

What did every child learn? 20

What happened if you got sick? 21

What would you eat? 22

Who would wash the dishes? 22

Were there special tricks for catching fish? 23

What did boys have to learn? 24

How would you make a dugout canoe? 25

What did girls have to learn? 26

What was the hardest thing a boy had to do? 28

Who were picked to be special warriors? 29

Why did the Wampanoag burn parts of the forest? 30

How would you know when to plant the corn? 31

Who took care of the fields? 31

How did Squanto help the Pilgrims? 33

How would you keep food from spoiling? 34

Did children have to work? 35
Would you have fun? 36
Would you have a pet? 38
What was the Wampanoag religion? 39
What was a sachem? 40
Who was Massasoit? 41
How did Squanto help make peace? 42
What would you do if your village was attacked? 43
Why were there so many trails? 44
What would you carry on a trip? 46
Would you meet Indians from other tribes? 47
What animals would you hunt for? 49
Why would you throw beaver bones back into the water? . . 50
How would you build a bear trap? 51
What was the big deer hunt? 52
What would you do on a stormy winter day? 53
Who came to the First Thanksgiving? 56
What happened when more and more English settlers came? 58
Do the Wampanoag live differently today? 60
FIND OUT MORE 62

Introduction

If you sailed down the coast of New England at the time of Columbus, what do you think you would see? A wild land where almost nobody lived?

No, you'd see a land full of people! As you sailed south, you'd see more and more villages with neat cornfields and green gardens. And there'd be another surprise: The Indians who lived there were taller and healthier than people who lived in Europe.

NEW ENGLAND

Atlantic Ocean

Nantucket

Martha's Vineyard

Long Island, New York

For almost a hundred years, that's what Europeans saw when they came to New England to fish and trade with the Native Americans. After they got their fish and furs, they sailed back home to Europe.

But that all changed on a cold winter's day in 1620, when the Pilgrims landed in Plymouth, Massachusetts. They hadn't come to trade — they had come to stay.

Whose land had the Pilgrims come to? It was the land of the Wampanoag (wamp-a-NO-ag) Indians. In fact, the Pilgrims built their houses where a Wampanoag village had stood a few years earlier. And it was a Wampanoag named Squanto who helped the Pilgrims survive their first two years.

Who were the Wampanoag people? How did they live before the Europeans came? What was it like to be a Wampanoag boy or girl? And what happened when the Europeans arrived? This book tells you all about it. For after 1620, America changed forever.

**When you see words in color, look in the
back of the book to find out more.**

Who were the Wampanoag Indians?

Wampanoag means **People of the East**. They lived along the coast of Massachusetts and Rhode Island, where their ancestors had lived for thousands of years.

The Wampanoag people were farmers. So every year, they moved to their summer villages, where each family grew its own corn, squash, and beans. Families also fished and dug for clams, and hunted in the forest. Everyone worked hard to make sure there'd be enough food for the long winter ahead.

What did the Wampanoag think of the Europeans?

The Europeans who came to trade must have looked very strange to the Wampanoag. They were dirty and they wore lots of odd clothes, even in the summer. Also, they had hair covering part of their faces! Indians didn't have beards. And unlike the Europeans, who thought bathing was bad for you, Indians were very clean.

But the Europeans did have iron kettles and knives and beautiful glass beads the Indians wanted. So they traded with the Europeans, who wanted fur pelts the Indians had. But when the trading was finished, the Wampanoag made sure the Europeans left on their ships.

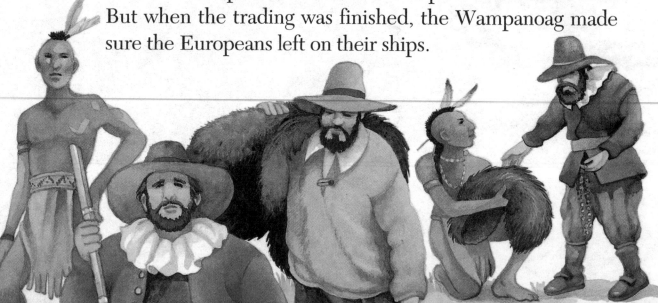

Who was Squanto?

Squanto was a Wampanoag warrior who was kidnapped by English sailors in 1614. They took him to Spain and sold him as a slave. After he was freed, he lived in England, where he learned to speak English.

When Squanto finally found a ship to take him home, he'd been gone for five years. As he sailed down the New England coast, he was horrified. Where were all the people? All he saw were broken-down villages and fields full of weeds.

When he reached his own village of Patuxet, he found out that his family and everyone in his village were dead from a great sickness.

Only Squanto was left.

What was the great sickness?

Imagine if a strange sickness came to your town and killed almost everyone you knew — your family, your friends, your neighbors. That's what happened in 1616 to Indians living on the New England coast. Often so many died, there was nobody left to bury the bodies.

As the great sickness spread down the coast, village after village lay empty, skulls and bones scattered on the ground. Only those living farther inland were spared. By 1619, most of the coastal Indians were dead.

Nobody today knows for sure what the great sickness was. But we do know that it was brought by the Europeans. They brought many terrible new diseases, such as smallpox and measles.

Why were the diseases from Europe different?

Today we know that when animals and people live close together, a disease can jump from animals to humans. Measles comes from cows, and flu from birds like ducks and chickens. Smallpox comes from cows, horses, and camels. Europeans had lots of cows, horses, and chickens, so their bodies had built up immunity to the diseases caused by these animals.

But Indians living in North America didn't have cows and horses and chickens. So they had never had those diseases before the Europeans came.

Where did the Wampanoag live?

Most of the year, the Wampanoag lived in villages near the sea. Each family had its own small round house, called a *wetu* (WE-too).

How to build a wetu:

1. Put one end of the poles into the ground. Then bend the poles and tie them together.
2. Cover the poles with grass **mats**. In cold weather, add sheets of bark on top of the mats.

A hole was made in the ceiling so smoke from your fire could get out. When it rained, you pulled a mat over the hole.

Wampanoag houses were warm and dry, even in rainstorms. In fact, the Pilgrims said that wetus were warmer than their own English houses!

After the fall harvest, everyone moved back to their winter village. Here you would live in a **longhouse** with your family and your cousins and uncles and aunts and grandparents.

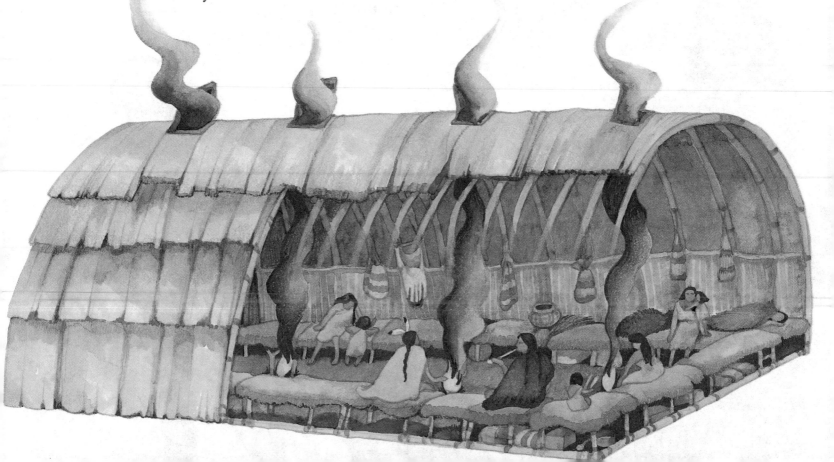

What would you wear?

Almost everyone wore a breechcloth, like the boy in this picture. It was a long, narrow piece of deerskin.

To put it on, you'd tuck it between your legs and pull the ends up under your belt so the flaps hung down in front and back. Younger boys didn't wear anything in the summer. They didn't start wearing breechcloths until they were ten.

Here's what you'd wear on a summer day.

If it got cold outside, you'd wrap yourself in a big piece of deerskin and fasten it on one shoulder. And you'd put on your **leggings** and **moccasins**. When it got really, really cold, you'd also put on your raccoon- or beaver-skin robe.

Would you have long hair?

Children had short hair until they were about sixteen.

Women wore their hair *really* long — sometimes down to their waist. They'd braid it, or wear it in a kind of ponytail.

Men spent a lot of time on their hair. Some wore it long. Others **shaved** most of it off, leaving only a patch of hair. The most popular style was a strip of hair running down the center of the head. The hair was **cut** short, and the men put paint and bear fat in it to make it stand straight up.

How would you take a bath?

You wouldn't use a bathtub — you'd go to a sweat lodge. And you'd bring your whole family!

First, your parents poured water on some hot rocks in the middle of the floor. That made the room nice and steamy and hot.

After leaving your clothes outside, you'd all crowd into the sweat lodge. While you sat on wooden benches, you'd be singing and talking and having a good time. The longer you sat, the more you sweated. After an hour, everyone ran outside and jumped into the pond or stream next to the sweat lodge.

Were parents strict?

Children were loved and watched over by everyone in their village. Parents never hit or yelled at their children.

The Pilgrims thought Wampanoag children were spoiled. Wampanoag parents wanted their children to play and explore, so they could learn how to take care of themselves. Pilgrim children had to stop playing when they were seven and start working like adults.

And Wampanoag children were allowed to roam the village and woods by themselves. The Pilgrims never let their children go very far away on their own.

What did every child learn?

You learned never to complain, no matter how bad things got. Sometimes parents tossed their naked children into the snow, and then quickly put them by the warm fire. It was only a game, but it helped make them tough.

You also learned to be honest. If you lied, nobody would respect you.

What happened if you got sick?

If you got sick, your mother would give you some medicine she made from special plants. Skunk cabbage was good for toothaches. If you had a sore throat, you'd chew on gum from the white pine tree.

You might also go to the sweat lodge. The Wampanoag believed that sweating helped make you well.

If you were *really* sick though, it was time to ask the pow-waw man for help. He was a very important man, because it was believed that he had magical powers to control the spirit world. Your family would pay him, just as we pay doctors today. It was his job to get rid of the angry spirits that were thought to make you sick.

What would you eat?

There was always a big pot of stewed corn and beans cooking on the fire. If your mother had some fish or meat, she'd cut it up and throw it in. Or she might put in some nuts or squash or even turtle meat. You never knew for sure, but it was always delicious.

In the morning, the whole family ate together. You'd fill your wooden bowl with hot stew and eat it with a clamshell spoon. The rest of the day, everyone ate whenever they felt hungry.

Of course you'd eat lots of other things, too — like corn cakes and roasted fish. In the summer, you'd eat the wild blueberries and strawberries that grew in the meadows.

You had clear, sweet water to drink. Sometimes you would have juice made from fruits, or tea made from berries and herbs.

Who would wash the dishes?

Nobody! The Wampanoag just wiped their **bowls** and put them away for the next meal.

Were there special tricks for catching fish?

The Wampanoag were great fishermen. They fished in the ocean as well as the streams and ponds. Sometimes they fished by themselves using only a hook and line or a spear. Other times they worked in groups, using huge **nets**.

One trick for catching lots of fish was to build a fence across the stream using sticks placed closely together. You left one small opening for the fish to swim through. That caused a *big* fish traffic jam. While all the fish were stuck waiting for their turn to swim through the opening, it was easy for the Indians to spear them or scoop them up in nets.

What did boys have to learn?

Men were hunters, warriors, and fishermen. So that's what boys learned to be, too.

You started shooting a bow and arrow when you were about two. After a while, you'd be good enough to go rabbit hunting. Older boys played dodging games, where they shot stick "arrows" at one another. This helped you if you became a warrior, because you'd be good at jumping around and avoiding being hit by enemy arrows.

You'd also learn how to make traps for catching bears, turkeys, and deer. And you'd learn to imitate birdcalls for hunting ducks and geese.

You would have fun helping your father build a dugout canoe.

How would you make a dugout canoe?

First, you chopped down a big pine or oak tree. Then, you cut off the branches and the bark. The log was split into two long pieces.

You burned out the inside of the log. Then you chipped away the soft, burned wood with a big clamshell.

The ends were rounded, and the canoe was smoothed with a rough stone.

It took a man about ten days to make a dugout canoe. When he was done, he'd go back to the village to get help carrying the heavy canoe to the water.

What did girls have to learn?

Girls learned to do what their mothers did.

The most important thing you learned was how to grow corn and beans and squash. Without them, your family might starve. At harvesttime, your mother would show you how to save the best seeds for next year's planting.

You'd also learn how to weave the grass mats used for building your house. And you'd make **baskets** and clay **cooking pots**.

Women did all the cooking, too. Before the dried corn was cooked, it had to be ground into cornmeal. So you'd learn how to do that.

You'd also learn to be a great swimmer. All children were taught when they were about two years old. Your parents might start by dropping you in the water! Soon you'd learn to dive and swim underwater and play games with the other children.

What was the hardest thing a boy had to do?

When a boy was about eleven, he was given an important test.

First he was blindfolded. Then his father or uncle took him deep into the forest and left him. Here the boy spent the whole winter with only a knife, a hatchet, and his **bow and arrows**. Nobody came to see him or help him. The boy had to hunt for his own food and build his own shelter. He had been well trained by then, so he knew what to do.

At the end of the winter, his father came back to get him. If the boy had done well, there was a big celebration with lots of dancing and good eating. For the boy had taken the first steps toward becoming a man.

Who were picked to be special warriors?

Only the strongest and smartest boys were chosen to become special warriors, called *pniesog* (pa-NEE-sog).

If you were chosen, you would leave your family and train with older warriors. To toughen you, they'd make you run through thorny bushes — often while hitting you with sticks on your bare legs. You'd also learn to go without eating for long periods.

Hardest of all was drinking a bitter juice that made you throw up blood. You'd drink it again and again, even if you almost fainted. You kept on drinking it until it finally stopped making you sick.

The pniesog were fearless warriors — one *pniese* (pa-NEES) would chase a hundred men. They were the chief's bodyguards and advisers. And they were respected for their wisdom and kindness.

Why did the Wampanoag burn parts of the forest?

The Wampanoag knew that deer liked to eat the new plants that grew after a fire. So they burned the bushes on their hunting grounds and left the big trees. That way they knew there'd be lots of deer.

With no bushes to hide in, the deer were also easier to spot. That made it easier to hunt them.

The Europeans were amazed to see how open much of the forest was. They said it looked like a park, not a wild forest.

How would you know when to plant the corn?

In the spring, you would watch the leaves on the white oak trees. When the leaves had grown as big as mouse ears, it was time to plant the corn.

Who took care of the fields?

Women were the farmers, so they took care of the fields. But the children helped. Together they planted the seeds, weeded, and picked the crops.

One of the biggest problems was keeping wild animals away:

- Crows wanted to eat the corn seeds.
- Blackbirds wanted to eat the tiny new plants.
- Raccoons wanted to eat the green corn.
- Woodchucks wanted to eat the squashes.
- And just about *everybody* wanted to eat the ripe yellow corn.

That's why there were special watchers in the fields. You'd sit high up on a wooden tower. The minute you spotted an intruder, you'd hoot and holler and throw stones. You might even kill the animal — that was all right. But never, never could you kill a crow. The Wampanoag believed that the crow was a sacred bird because it brought the first corn and bean seeds as a gift from Kiehtan (KEE-ah-tuhn), the Creator.

How did Squanto help the Pilgrims?

The wheat and peas the Pilgrims brought from England didn't grow very well in America. But the corn, beans, and squash they got from the Wampanoag *did* grow well. And it was Squanto who showed the Pilgrims how to grow them together, Wampanoag-style.

Corn, beans, and squash were called the Three Sisters because they helped one another grow. The corn helped the bean plant climb up its stalk to get sunshine. The bean plant made the soil better. And the squash, with its big leaves, shaded the soil and kept it damp.

Squanto also showed the Pilgrims a special trick. After you dug a hole in the soil, you'd put a small fish into the hole before dropping the seeds in. As the fish rotted, it became "food" for the plants and made them grow better.

How would you keep food from spoiling?

There were no refrigerators or freezers in those days. But the Wampanoag knew how to keep the food from spoiling. They dried it!

After the corn was picked, the women and children put it out in the sun. Dry corn lasted for years.

You had to cut the squashes and pumpkins into long, thin strips before you hung them up to dry. You'd also dry strawberries, blueberries, and nuts in the sun.

Fish and meat were cut into pieces and dried over a slow smoky fire. The smoke kept the flies away and made the food taste delicious. Sometimes they used the **smokehouse**, where meat could smoke all night long or when the weather was rainy.

After all the food had been dried, it was put into baskets and stored in large pits in the ground. That kept the food safe until you were ready to eat it in the winter.

Did children have to work?

Yes, children worked, too. There were lots of things for them to do.

- They carried water from the stream.
- They dug for clams.
- They caught rabbits and muskrats in traps.
- They gathered firewood.
- They picked wild strawberries and cranberries.
- They dug up clay along the riverbank for making pots.
- And they caught eels in the stream by pushing them out of the mud with their bare feet and grabbing them before they wiggled away.

Would you have fun?

There was plenty of time for having fun. In the summer, you'd run races, play ball games, swim, and play in the woods. The Wampanoag loved to dance, too. They danced at all their festivals — or even just to cheer someone up!

In the winter, everybody's favorite game was snow snakes. You'd all take turns throwing a long, thin stick down a track. The stick wiggled like a snake when you threw it, so it was hard to throw it far. Whoever threw the snow snake the farthest down the track won.

A ball game similar to **soccer** always had big crowds, especially if one tribe was playing another. The game was played on the beach, with the two goal posts almost a mile apart. You couldn't recognize who any of the players were because their faces were covered with war paint. But even though they played rough and sometimes got hurt, they had a great time. After the game, everyone celebrated together at a big feast.

Would you have a pet?

Yes, you'd have dogs — maybe as many as five or six. The dogs were small and looked a lot like foxes.

Dogs were an important part of your family. When a stranger or a dangerous animal came near your house, they'd bark and warn you. They also guarded the fields so that raccoons or woodchucks didn't get the chance to eat your family's vegetables.

When you went duck hunting, the dogs lay quietly in the canoe until you gave them a signal — sometimes just with your hand. Then they'd leap into the water to get the duck you had just shot down.

The dogs were very fast in the snow. They weighed so little that they could run on top of the snow's crust without falling through. On moose hunts, the dogs helped chase down a moose until it got tired from running in the deep snow. Then the hunters could easily kill it.

What was the Wampanoag religion?

The Wampanoag believed that everything on Earth had its own sacred spirit — people, animals, plants, even rocks. They also believed that if you showed the spirits respect, they would help you.

That's why hunters prayed to the animal's spirit for help. If the hunt was successful, everyone celebrated. And the hunters thanked the animal for allowing itself to be killed so the hunters' families could have food.

The Wampanoag believed that their spirits went to live with Kiehtan, the Creator, after they died. But murderers, thieves, and liars were not allowed into heaven. Like ghosts, they had to wander the earth, causing illnesses and trouble for the living.

What was a sachem?

A *sachem* (SAY-chum) was the leader of a village. He decided when to go to war and when to make peace. And he made other important decisions. But he didn't make them until he first talked to the wise elders in his village.

If your parents needed more land for growing food, the sachem would give it to them. If two families had an argument, the sachem helped work it out.

People in the village paid a kind of tax to the sachem. But they didn't pay the tax with money — they paid it with corn, squash, fish, meat, and furs. That made the sachem rich, but he didn't keep it all to himself. He gave most of it to people who needed help.

After a sachem died, his oldest son became the new sachem. If the sachem had no sons, his daughter might become sachem. Both Nantucket Island and Martha's Vineyard were once ruled by powerful "queen sachems."

Who was Massasoit?

Massasoit was the sachem and leader of the Wampanoag people in Squanto's time. His real name was Massasoit Ousamequin, which means "Chief Yellow Feather."

When the Pilgrims arrived in 1620, things were not going well for Massasoit. Most of his people had died in the great sickness, and many villages lay empty. So many Wampanoag warriors were dead that their old enemy the Narragansetts thought it was safe to attack the Wampanoag and steal their land.

After Squanto had come back from England, he told every-one about the powerful English and their big cities. He also had some advice for Massasoit: If you make peace with the English, your enemies will be afraid to attack you, because they will be afraid the English will fight on your side.

Massasoit was a great leader. He was very smart and he knew how to listen to ordinary people. Although he was a brave warrior, he always tried to work things out rather than go to war.

And he did make peace with the Pilgrims.

How did Squanto help make peace?

Massasoit wanted the Pilgrims to help if the Wampanoag were attacked. The Pilgrims wanted to live in peace on Wampanoag land. So they decided to sign a peace treaty.

But Massasoit didn't speak English, and the Pilgrims didn't speak the Wampanoag language. How could they talk to each other? Through Squanto! He had learned English when he was captured and lived in England.

With Squanto's help, Massasoit and the Pilgrims made peace — a peace that lasted fifty years, until Massosoit died.

What would you do if your village was attacked?

If your village was attacked, the women and children would run into the marshes or forest and hide. The men would stay and fight.

It was important to hide quickly, because sometimes the enemy captured the women and children. If that happened to you, you would have to go to their village and live there, maybe for the rest of your life.

Some Wampanoag built tall fences around their villages to protect them from attacks.

Why were there so many trails?

There were no cars in those days, and the Native Americans living in New England had no horses. So unless you could get there by canoe, you walked.

That's why there were so many trails. Runners with important messages used them. Indians from other tribes coming to trade used them. Families moving to their summer homes used them. Children out berry picking used them. Everybody used them.

The trails were easy to find, too. Indians had walked on them for thousands of years, wearing some paths down until they were twelve inches deep. And you always knew you'd find water to drink, because the trails were put near streams and ponds.

Today, we have roads and highways where many of the Wampanoag trails used to be. But there are still a few places left deep in the woods, where, if you look very hard, you can see parts of the ancient trails.

What would you carry on a trip?

If you were going on a trip, you'd bring along a warm deer-skin cape and some leggings. And, of course, you'd take your moccasins. But you wouldn't wear them unless you got cold.

You'd carry two special stones in a bag tied to your belt. When you wanted to make a fire, you'd strike them to make sparks. Pretty soon you'd have a good fire going.

For food, you'd carry some ground corn, called *noohkik* (no-kick). And you'd carry your wooden bowl.

You'd also bring your stone knife, tied to a string around your neck. If you were a boy or a man, you'd bring your bow and arrows, too. A man would bring his **pipe** and some tobacco.

As you walked along the trail, you always hoped you'd meet somebody, so you could stop and have a good chat.

Would you meet Indians from other tribes?

Indians from other tribes might come to your village to trade. Before they started trading, the men sat down and shared a friendly smoke of tobacco. If your visitors were from another New England tribe, you'd have an easy time understanding them. All New England Indians spoke a similar language.

You also met people from other tribes in the spring, when they gathered at the big waterfalls. That was the best place

to catch the salmon and other fish as they swam upriver to lay their eggs. Your father might be fishing next to someone from an enemy tribe, but it didn't matter. At the falls, everyone was at peace.

All day, the men were busy spearing fish or catching them in nets. The women and children dried and smoked the fish, and packed it into baskets. If your father caught a sturgeon, there'd be food for your whole village that winter. Some sturgeons weighed eight hundred pounds!

What animals would you hunt for?

If you were a boy, you'd learn how to hunt all of the animals in this picture. Can you name them?

Answer: Deer, moose, bear, otter, beaver, duck, rabbit, squirrel, raccoon, and turkey.

Why would you throw beaver bones back into the water?

Beavers were killed for their meat and for their warm fur. But their bones were never thrown to the dogs. That would have shown disrespect. Then the beaver's spirit might have come back to punish you.

Instead, you would return to the place where you had caught the beaver. There you would throw the bones back into the waters where the beaver once swam.

How would you build a bear trap?

If you were a boy, you'd learn how to build a trap like the one in this picture. As soon as the bear started to eat the bait, the pole holding the bait tipped over. Then the logs and stones fell down and killed the bear.

The Wampanoag used almost every part of the bear. Skins were made into clothing and blankets for cold winter nights. Bear meat and bear fat were special treats. You'd use bear fat to "butter" your corn cakes. And everyone rubbed bear fat on themselves to keep the insects from biting.

What was the big deer hunt?

In the fall, the big deer hunt began.

Men, women, and children all joined in. There might be two or three hundred people. They would all go to the hunting ground.

First, everyone helped build two brush fences in the shape of a large V. The fences might be a mile long. Then, some people formed a long line at the wide end between the fences. As they walked, they made a lot of noise, so that the frightened deer ran ahead of them. When the deer got to the narrow end of the V, they were trapped. That made it easy for the hunters to shoot them with their bows and arrows.

After the deer were killed, the women carried them to the hunting camp to skin them and cut up the meat. When all the meat was packed, it was time to return to the winter village.

What would you do on a stormy winter day?

Imagine this: It's a cold winter morning, and the wind is howling outside. Your mother tells you to go out and get some more wood for the fire. While you put on your moccasins and warm fur cape, your sister is already back from the spring with a **bucket** of water.

Your mother is busy cutting up the meat from the squirrels you shot yesterday with your bow and arrow. She drops it into the stew pot and adds some dried wild onions. Already there's a delicious smell in the longhouse from the other families' cooking pots.

As your baby sister watches from her **cradle board**, your mother and older sister begin to grind corn. You and your father start making wooden bowls. Carefully, you lift a hot coal from the fire and put it on the wood. After the burned wood has cooled, you scrape it away and burn the wood some more. When your bowl is finished, you rub it with bear fat and polish it with a beaver tooth.

Whenever you feel hungry, you eat some hot stew or a freshly baked corn cake. A stranger is passing through your village, so your family invites him to stay for the night.

In the evening, everyone gathers around your grandfather, who is the village storyteller. As the fire crackles, he tells the story of Moshup, the giant who created the island of Martha's Vineyard. Moshup was so strong he could pick a whale out of the sea, throw it against the cliffs, and cook it for his supper. It is said that when fog covers Cape Cod, it is really the smoke from Moshup's pipe.

When your family is ready to go to sleep, they give the visitor your place on the family bed. You sleep on the floor, but you don't mind, because you're warm under your bearskin blanket. The last thing you hear as you doze off is your parents and relatives singing themselves to sleep.

Who came to the First Thanksgiving?

By the fall, the Pilgrims had so much corn, squash, and beans that there was enough food for the winter. Now nobody would starve. That's why they decided to have a big harvest festival — our first Thanksgiving.

Who was invited? Surely their friend Squanto, who lived right there with the Pilgrims. And also Hobbamock, who was Massasoit's ambassador at Plymouth. He probably brought his wife and children. The Pilgrims also invited the great Massasoit. They knew that without his help, they would never have survived.

But Massasoit didn't come alone. He brought along ninety of his men! The Pilgrims were worried. How could they feed all their new guests? Massasoit had the answer: His men went out hunting and brought back five deer.

The harvest festival lasted for three days, during which everyone ate and ate and had a good time. The Pilgrims marched in a parade and fired their noisy guns into the air. The children played games. And the Wampanoag danced in a long line and sang their ancient songs.

58

What happened when more and more English settlers came?

The English settlers started taking the Wampanoag hunting and fishing grounds. They built their houses on land that the Wampanoag had cleared for themselves. And the English settlers let their pigs and horses run all over Wampanoag fields and ruin the corn and beans.

Metacomet was Massasoit's son. He was called King Philip by the English. After he became the Wampanoag leader, he decided to start a war to get rid of the English settlers. Other Indians joined him.

King Philip's War lasted one terrible, bloody year. Metacomet's warriors attacked towns and killed the settlers.

The English soldiers killed the Indians and burned their houses and food. But Metacomet did not have enough warriors to defeat all the English soldiers. By winter, most of the Indians were starving and homeless.

When Metacomet was killed, the war ended. Almost half of the English settlers were now dead. And most of the Wampanoag villages had been destroyed. The Wampanoag who were still alive were scattered throughout the land.

But even though the war was over, the British soldiers decided to hunt down the Wampanoag and other Indians. Many were caught and killed. Others, including Metacomet's son, were sold as slaves in the Caribbean. Those who fled to Cape Cod and nearby islands joined the Wampanoag communities that had not fought in the war.

After King Philip's War, life was very hard for the Wampanoag. They had lost their land and their freedom. And now they were treated as conquered people.

Do the Wampanoag live differently today?

The Wampanoag no longer live the way their ancestors did. Like other Americans today, they have cars and TVs and computers. And they live in modern houses, not in wetus. But they still honor their tribal traditions.

Most Wampanoag live in Massachusetts — in towns like Mashpee on Cape Cod and Gay Head on Martha's Vineyard. Every fall, they celebrate the Green Corn Festival and the Cranberry Festival, just as the Wampanoag did long ago.

For many years there was nobody left who could speak the Wampanoag language. But today some Wampanoag are working to bring their language back. This is hard to do because the Wampanoag never wrote down their language. So there are no books to tell you what words meant or how to pronounce them.

Luckily, in 1663, a minister named John Eliot and a group of Indians, led by Job Nesutan, translated the Bible into the Wampanoag language.

Today that Bible is helping the Wampanoag to learn their old language again — the same language that Massasoit and Squanto spoke when they first met the Pilgrims so long ago.

Here are some words in Massachusett, which is the name of the language that the Wampanoag spoke:

kwe — **hello**	*nahom* — **turkey**
atuk — **deer**	*namas* — **fish**
nipi — **water**	*ausup* — **raccoon**
moos — **moose**	*attitash* — **blueberries**

Here's how to count to four:

nequt — **one**   *neese* — **two**   *nish* — **three**   *yau* — **four**

FIND OUT MORE . . .

page 8 People of the East Because they lived in the most eastern part of the country, the Wampanoag were the first to see the sunrise every day. They are also called People of the Dawn, or People of the First Light, or People of the Breaking Day.

page 12 immunity Immunity means protection from disease. It is the job of the immune system in your body to attack germs that make you sick. If you are exposed to certain germs over a long period of time, your immune system gets much better at destroying these germs. Then your body will have immunity from those diseases.

page 13 mats The outside mats were made of cattail leaves that women sewed together. These mats were big — about five feet wide and ten feet long.

Women also wove mats from grasses called bulrushes. These were hung on the walls inside the wetus. Often they were decorated with beautiful paintings.

page 15 longhouse Some longhouses were so big that ten families could live there. Other longhouses had only a few families.

Each family had its own section in the longhouse with sleeping benches, storage places, and a fire pit.

page 17 leggings Leggings were made from soft deerskin. The women used needles made of animal bones, and thread made of animal tendons to sew the leggings. (Tendon is the stretchy tissue that attaches a bone to muscle. It is also called sinew.)

page 17 moccasins Moccasins were cut from one large piece of deerskin or from stronger moose hide.

A soft sole was sewn to the hide. The moccasins were tied at the ankle with a deerskin strap. Each moccasin could be worn on either foot so they would wear out evenly.

page 18 shaved and cut hair There were no scissors or razors. Hair was cut with knives made of animal bones, antlers, sharp shells, or stones such as shale. Some men pulled out hair from the roots, one by one, to make part of their head completely bald.

page 22 bowls The Wampanoag made bowls in many sizes. Small bowls were used as cups and spoons.

page 23 nets The Indians made nets from plant fibers, such as hemp, or fibers from the linden tree. To make a purse net like the one shown in the picture on this page, the fibers were woven into a net and a strip of wood was inserted along one side for the frame. The frame was bent and tied onto a long stick. With a purse net, you could get lots of fish, not just one at a time.

page 26 baskets The women and girls made baskets of all sizes, some square, some round. Many were woven using stiff grasses; corn husks; hemp fibers; and bark peeled from logs cut from maple, oak, hickory, and ash trees. The bark had to be cut into strips and soaked in water before the weaving could begin.

page 26 cooking pots To make the cooking pots, the women and girls used clay from the banks of a stream. They added crushed stones, burned shells, or plant fibers to the clay as they kneaded and shaped it into pots. Sometimes they made beautiful designs on the outside of the pot, using the edge of a shell or a stick shaped like a fork.

page 28 bow and arrows Wampanoag bows were longer than those used by Indians in the West. Men used wooden bows that were five to six feet long. Favorite woods were ash, oak, witch hazel, and hickory. The bow strings were made of moose sinew.

Arrows were tipped with sharp arrowheads made from stone. The men spent many hours in the longhouse during the winter chipping large stones into arrowheads and tools such as hatchets (also called tomahawks), like the one shown on page 9.

A hunter carried his arrows in a quiver that was strapped to his chest. Some quivers were made of wood, some of animal skins.

page 34 smokehouse A smokehouse was like a small longhouse that was open at both ends. You can see one in the picture on page 9.

page 36 soccer Today we play soccer with a round leather ball filled with air. The ball used by the Wampanoag was not quite round. It was made of deerskin and stuffed with deer hair. Now, only the goalkeeper in soccer may touch the ball. In the Indians' game, players kicked and sometimes ran with the ball.

page 37 picture, top right These children are having fun pulling up yellow pond lilies. They put the lilies in the basket to take home. Their mother will roast the roots, which are good to eat. The Indians also liked to eat wild groundnuts, strawberries, blueberries, and blackberries. Groundnuts, which are about the size of a hen's egg, helped the Pilgrims survive the winter of 1623.

page 46 pipe The Wampanoag, like many other Indian peoples, smoked pipes as a sign of friendship.

Pipes were smoked at religious ceremonies and when making peace treaties. Wampanoag men grew their own tobacco and tended the fields themselves. (Women did all the other farmwork.)

Pipes were made of wood or stone. Some were decorated with designs or carvings of animals. Some were as long as two feet! Massasoit's pipe, shown in the picture on page 43, had a carving of a bear on the bowl.

page 53 bucket What kind of container did the Indians use to carry water? A clay pot was heavy — not the best choice. Water would leak through a basket. What else was there? Tree bark! Bark from the birch tree was especially good. It was very lightweight and could be folded and shaped into trays, cups, boxes, bags, and pails for carrying water. Often the pieces of bark were first dipped into hot water to make them easier to fold.

page 54 cradle board Before a baby was born, his father built a cradle board. It had a smooth, flat, wooden back and a soft pouch to keep the baby warm.

Once the baby was strapped into the cradle board, its mother could carry him on her back as she moved around.

She could also hang the cradle board on a branch while she worked in the fields. Babies went everywhere with their mothers, so the babies always felt like they were part of things.

You may want to read these books, too.

Tapenum's Day
A Wampanoag Indian Boy
in Pilgrim Times

by KATE WATERS
Photographs by
RUSS KENDALL

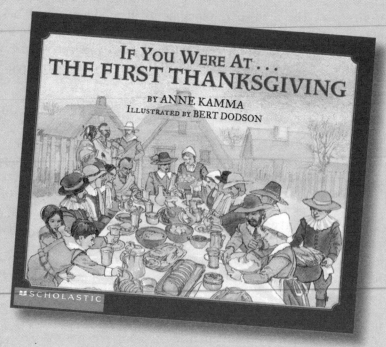

IF YOU WERE AT . . .
THE FIRST THANKSGIVING
BY ANNE KAMMA
ILLUSTRATED BY BERT DODSON

SCHOLASTIC